Counsel

Kelley White

Acknowledgments

"The Beginning" was included on www.poetsagainstthewar.uk

"Abundance" was published in *Desert Voices*

"Allowance" was published in *The Eclectic Muse* (Canada)

"Art of the Americas" has been accepted for publication by *femme,* and by PFS Post (online)

"August" has been accepted to appear in *Defect Cult,* Red Hand Press

"Azrael" was published online at www.comrades.org.uk

"Behind the Dog Army" has been published *Pitchfork*

"Chordae" was published by *The Broadkill Review* and was nominated for a Pushcart Prize and was included in the Broadkill Press Key Chapbook Series Chapbook *Ice Solstice*

"Cinder" has been published in *Curbside Review*

"Code" has been published in *Seeding the Snow*

"Counsel" appeared online at *Tattoo Highway*

"Cupboard" and "Economy" were been published online by *Tin Lustre Mobile*

"Daughter, each dawn" has been accepted for publication by *Broadkill Review* and for Broadkill

Press Key Chapbook Series *Ice Solstice*

"Debt" has been accepted for publication online by *Ken*Again*

"Dispatches," "Matins," "Sieve," "Was it supposed to be" and "What is holier than dust?" were published in *Parting Gifts*

"Exercise" was accepted to appear at *High Horse* on-line

"Fib" and "Fight the River" appeared on-line at *Ken*again*

"If I have a chance I'll show you this one thing" was published at *Burningword.com*

"If each feather is perfect what/then is the bird?" and "It is done" were published on-line at

Tamaphyr Mountain Poetry

"I sang in wind" was accepted for *Ken*Again* on-line

"Jeu pardis" was published in *Big Scream/Nada Press*

"Kite" was accepted to appear online at *Covert Poetics*

"Koana" was published in *Small Brushes/Adept Press*

"Labor" has been accepted by *SNReview*

"Long Distance" received First Honorable Mention in the 16th Annual Free Verse Contest (Robert Penn Warren Awards) and is to be published in *Anthology of New England Writers*

"Lost Poem" has been accepted by *Ken*Again* on-line and appeared online at *Concelebratory Shoehorn Review*

"Lull" has been accepted by *The Deronda Review*

"Maiden" was published in *Mojo Risin'*

"The Maiden Flight of the Bumblebee/The Mating Flight of the Drone" was held for *Labour of Love*

"May a river," was published in *Opened Eyes*

"Myoclonus" appeared in *Hidden Oak* and in a slightly different version as "Between Living and Dreaming" in *Midwest Poetry Review*

"Nobody" appeared in *Poesy*

"Nothing" has been accepted to appear in *Lalitamba*

"Pray" appeared in *The Broadkill Review* and was included in *Ice Solstice* Broadkill Press Key   Chapbook Series

"Relinquish" has been accepted to appear in *Friends Journal*

"Show us the bottom of yesterday's grief" has been accepted by *Main Street Rag*

"Study Questions" appeared in *The Café Review*

"Todd" was accepted in a slightly different version for *Buckle &*

"Tremble at" appeared in *Erete's Bloom*

"Trust the Reader""appeared in *Hidden Oak*

"Waltz for Empty Arms" was published in C*offee Ground Breakfast*

"Wednesday" has been accepted to appear in *The Unrorean*

"What Aesha said about Lazarus, has been accepted by Scars Publications

"What insects know" has been accepted for publication by *Hingeonline*

"Whelk" has been accepted for publication by PFS post online

"Who are your dead?" was published in *The Dan River Anthology*

"Why have they broken the child's hands" was accepted for *Coupremine* on-line

"Will this one dance?" appeared online a *Hapa Nui*

"Worn" has been accepted for publication by *Arnazella Literary Arts Magazine*

"You are a river to our city," has been accepted *Mischief, Caprice, and Other Poetic Strategies*: *Writers at Work Anthology*

Daughter, each dawn

the pebbles of the riverbed
bathe in the roselight
and dance

their joy is mine

when I held your new palm

Contents

The Beginning

Ice creaks in the darkness. Birds huddle night.
Cries in the shadows. Stars fall in flight.

Allowance

What did you hide
under the stairs
and take out each night
after dark?

Who did you call
after midnight last year
and hang up on
the answering voice?

Why did you write in
the book of your loss
and then put it away
in a drawer?

Who did you miss
in the softness of light
after anger
had fallen away?

Where is the mountain
you're planning to climb
when daylight has
knitted to night?

Whose name will you speak
when you're trying to die?
Whose blessings
will you report?

Art of the Americas

i.
unhook the latch
blow off dust
lay on the table beneath a single dangling bulb
spine flat
slick leaves open
always to the tight black-lined woodcut
man on man
manu a manu
knife
blade
empty chest
heart beating overhead

ii.
It is said that Crazy Horse ate Custer's heart.
This is not true. Buffalo liver, perhaps.

iii.
pyramid
disinhearted
throw the rib-shell over the priest's shoulder

iv.
abyss

v.
this thing
this flabby old muscle

stilled
red and growing darker
fat encrusted
drying to tallow
gristle
in each chamber
one smooth green stone
marbled
like my eyes

vi.
ice arrest
watch
the saw cut
that grinding buzz
the dental whine

vii.
"hey babe,
I'll give you water,
I already had
my wine"
(wants a dollar,
give him four bits)

viii.
you won't answer
(the child had
no ear drum)

ix.
Henry carved a green stone heart
on a brass stand and marble base.

The children broke it.
No one confessed.
They were all punished.

x.
finger crook-and-pull
my own ribs
and still this hubbub

xi.
to become invisible
or rather:
the visible woman
clear plastic
head molded with Berry Crocker
hair
hips a little wide, perhaps
a babe in the womb
no

xii.
ectopia coridis
child with the heart
outside the chest
cordae
cordate
card
iac arrest
press
chest
repressed

xiii.
I will be this small stone you might carry,
the brass paperweight that warms
to your touch,
your mother's, yours.
Replace my wound
with a stone.
Carry the stone.
Live stone
cold.

Azrael

tired as
the dried up face
of an apple
left in October
Indian summer
heat

hot as
burning teeth
singed hair
marrow cry
beneath tomorrow's
broken voice

Behind the Dog Army

My mouth is a freezer full of frozen meat.
Your car has a lover.
She is a turtle, newly waxed, with a gift for flattery,
and the perfume of the sea. Her music makes
a light show against your walls.
Jonathan wears a 49er's cap but doesn't know
the city. My mouth is empty.
The dogs have dug new holes in the permafrost.
They wish to worship Siberia.
That one, she needs her head examined.
You telling me.
The night horses of invention live through eternity.
Ease me against the bricks.
Teach my tongue to lick happiness, Jellybean,
old girl, you many yet learn dogged
verse. Melting circumcision.
The veracity of crows. Go, tell Jeroboam:
Let the trees dance new haired in the doglit night.
Let them find the frozen harvest
forgotten in the snow.

Chordae

Aren't the places we receive the stigmata
    also the eyes by which we see love?

I wanted to be a tree, walking
    full of all the animated communities that were
    my cells, osteoblasts laying down new bone as osteoclasts
     chewed away another mesa, osteocytes
     secure as coral in their lacunae
     bathed in a sea of blood
I saw the alveolae, monkeys laughing
  in my branches, pulling down
    the fruited O's of air
and the clicking tautness, this heart my harp, the kiss and release
    of valves, mitral and tricuspid, chambers full and empty
    the music of the chordae thrummed

and I thought of us joined by this flap of flesh
like Cheng and Eng, simple blood and skin, and of how easily
    the connection could be severed
yet they stayed conjoined even when one pumped poison
    to the other's liver

I felt your cells rising, like seed from the dandelion head blown
    by my wind and my music
but they danced the dance of those sexless deepsea creatures
    who moved in the hungry
    ghost dance of a scarf dropped in steam
    or slow ink moving through oil

their genitals a thousand, ten thousand, a hundred thousand
weapons, knives that cut and cut and cut
the other
and she who was most wounded was the female
she who must heal and bear
the young

Cinder

Ask the one tree that bends
    on a day when no wind blows.
Ask the skull of a bird that you find
    on your porch. Ask
the thrown brick and the iron held
    tight for burning.
Ask the still pool of water. Ask
    the larva beneath.

Take of their answers a prayer
    of forgetting. Make
of their whispers a carved ivory
    stone. Take of the winter
the shape of the water
    that cracks the still rock
in the face of your soul

Code

in the language of insects
    my name would be tree
to the bird I am "walks-without-wonder"
I am "heavy" and "noisy"
    to the ants on my walk
"once-a-week-rain" for my ivy

"mother who cries" the cat
    tells his dog friend
 "walks very slow" he replies
"always talking" breathes the
    telephone wire
"heavy sleep" whispers the window

Cold Snap

the night you left with no word
the windowglass cold on my face
the children stirred in the white bright night
and I turned on cold pale sheets

the knives sat bright and cold
as the pillow against my cheek
the water sat cold in the bedside glass
the summer was cold as faith

a man cried in the street
naked and shaking with chill
I asked for police and safety
with the turn of a cold blue wheel

and still I knew you'd gone
and you were not coming back
so by morning I packed my bags with snow
and left and forgot to laugh

Counsel

Here the message carved on the skin
of a sapling, here the secret stitched
on the back of a stone, here the whisper
woven into the river, the silence wrapped
in the white of a bone. Yesterday's twilight
sang to the birds of the highway, gentled
evening into the dark of the hill, quieted
dawn through the pinhole of Saturn,
weeping; pitied the housewife sweeping
without a broom. Read the conclusion
torn from the back of a sparrow, sing
the inscription bleeding down yesterday's
face; carry moonlight home to the doves
of the evening, wrap them with ribbons
rent from the bricks of disgrace. Root
them in sand with the skull of an osprey,
scrape it and grind with the claw
of a crone, bury it wrapped in the husk
of a deerchild, make the sign of the
hawk, mark the sign of the glove.

Watch for the heat that rises
before you see fire, summon the shout
that defines the morning with grief.
Dive for the merchants who cry out
for pearls and for amber. Beg for
the moment when cattle and ducklings
release. Uncover the seam that
was whittled from childhood. Speak

to the angel who brazens the sword
of the priest. Sustain the dance the silent
one has forgotten. Answer the hermit
who quickens the water and reeds.
Gather the remnant of crystal and vagabond
children. Teach them the lessons the
swallows engraved on a leaf. Unbind
your hair and caress the walls of the
fortress. Slip off the veils of your father's
beliefs.

Cupboard

here is my tent
    made of blankets and table
here is my dugout fort
    in the snowhill
here is my closet hung
    with warm clothes and shoe racks
here is my darkness
    beneath the bedclothes

here light comes rich
    with colors through darkness
here sounds are muffled
    and sweeter to hear
here I am held and I don't ask
    for holding
here I can listen
    to what I would hear

Dear Carrot,

your breath lies under the dirt
and above you are a flight of green angels still
sturdy enough to pull at the gate of ground;
and oh, surprise
that one might gain a sweet orange finger,
a button or
a dancing ginseng man;

raw you are sweeter than cooked
and the snap of my teeth
or the crack of the knife against
the butcher's block sings of winter
and the wonder of change;

overboiled, pureed,
we may suckle
to clear night sight,
even in our toothless,
grinning,
old baby mouths,

delight

Debt

I dreamed someone had pasted
large sheets of blotting
paper all over my door.
I peeled it off carefully
saving and rolling the pieces
of adhesive paper trying
to read the messages indented in
each corner. The mailman had placed
my mail above the door
and window frames but I was able
to climb upon a passing giant's back.
Inside the children were making
a collage of my poems. My daughter
said they were just substituting
something a little livelier
for my cardboard drafts. I woke
with the taste of old sugar in
my mouth. You'd left a check
in the mailbox for $4.54.
What you calculate you owe me
after six years of life together.

What insects know

is carved in rune sticks
sung time
dark rhythms
and deep sweet
undercurrenting sleep

Deliverance

the child enters the oven
and lays on the burning straw
her eyes see
the white light
in the click of the flame

the girl lies on ice
and whispers to the tightening darkness
her eyes see
the white light
in the silence of cold

the woman cups
a flame in her hands
and teaches it to dance
along her children's skin, holy
her eyes see
the white light
in the sinew of love

Dispatches

I would read a message in a broken tree
I would read a message in a spider's web
I would read a message in a ledge of stone
be open   be strong   grow old

Economy

or thorns
or an overturned bowl
or the calling of crows

or we took in a boarder
or an empty saddle bag
or nothing

or empty hands
or smoke
or the haunted door

or naughty
or laundry taken in
or a freckled paw

or a winter branch
or frog jelly
or the surprise of joy

Fib

one
plus one
the ram's horn
curls equals two plus
one equals three a pentangle
eight plus five, thirteen, the morning glory vine coils out
tender green shoots breach sky more heat new light quick nautilus
lays out slick chambers excrete new calcium accretes its self,
greater anteroom
the piglet's tail winds ecstatic
suckling curls clockwork
flagella
beating
home

Fight the River

that carries you reaching for branches
the river that carries your children too fast
the water that coldly caresses your bruises
the current that threatens to tear you to ice

lay back with your arms out and face to the sunlight
remember you carry a lightness of heart
lay back on your strong back and kick
your legs slowly if you taught your children

they also can float

Grave

That moment when gravity becomes repulsive
and you lift to watch your body from the ceiling bulb—
body, empty husk, body, only one life to climb
the spirit air, one shadow to shift and wait above—
See how she cries on the bed, see her two hands
lift to her mouth as if to pull the soul from her face,
but the soul does not hear, it has left her and lingers
with the souls of the ancestors, each with a finger
to her lips as the man pulls up his trousers and walks
away

If each feather is perfect what then is the bird?

as the fruit contains the flower
the full moon contains the new
the cricket's song contains silence
the vortex surrenders still
step into the space of rainfall
enter emptiness and wind
part the waterfall, surrender
seek the sustenance within

as the tree breaks from the rock face
as the cliff remembers ice
as a mother holds her children
air is hung with heavy clouds
take a coin against forgetting
take a seed to plant in fall
be a stem to leaf and flower
be the husk that held it all

If I have a chance I'll show you this one thing

to peel an orange in one continuous spiral
one perfect careful stripe of orange with just a fingernail
and thumb, lay the sweet fragrance onto hands
and into the room, put the fruit
one segment at a time
into your mouth, then rewind the peel
into a perfect globe, each edge remet and fit
to its brother whole, hollow, yes, emptied, but perfect still

I lay down in a cold clear stream

because I was torn and bleeding and I wanted
to feel ice. I lay down on a bed of dappled
pebbles and asked them to etch my nakedness
to stone. I lay down beneath a sky spun
with light and bird calls and tried to still
the thunder in my ears. I lay waiting for the ice
to save me. I asked water to carve me
to a bone flute that would sing my name
from the notch of a tree. I lay listening for
the snow melt on the broken mountain, for
the footfall of deer, for the bullet's song
when they bent their slender brown throats
to my mouth to drink

I sang in wind

and you did not hear me
I moved with the high leaves
and you did not see
dust in your road
the creak in your old gate
but you do not taste me
coldness, and you ask for heat

I bowed with the branches
at the coming thunder
still water, and the darkling deep
lightning, and the haze
of midsummer
you did not touch me
nor the meadow sweet

each blade of grass is companioned
each ant celebrates a feast
I alone call fullness empty
I alone make myself weep

It is done

Just today I saw the flames around the children
but they did not burn. I saw the sweetest honey
flowing from the beggar's hands and he was
smiling. Around the dead pigeon in the gutter
danced wings made of light. They flew with
the corpse and a sound like bells laughing. Clouds
parted that sacred sky. Children took the beggar's
hands and climbed ice to the sun. They left the flames
at my feet. I let my hair down. Burning, it hissed
with holy whispers. Full, I sing the eager breath
of stars. I lift my fingers as candles and sign holy
day holy day holy day

Jeu pardis

The sirens are circling my village at sunset.

Wires come undone overhead.
They sizzle and snap,
medusas in the evening fog.

My car stalls in highway traffic.
The children starve waiting
for a way to cross the street.

It is winter. An icicle has fallen through the heart of my only
relative.

You are waiting on the porch having at last added up
the times I called your number.
The sum has given
your bullets a name.

Labor

my body split open
like a stone and sang
a praisesong
to the mothers
cave gone light
with dawn

Kite

In the city of sorrow a child dances
between night and broken sidewalk.
He has made a bird of spidersilk and thorns.
It sails on a chain of morningglory vines. He laughs
the melody of tomorrow's blossoms
into the silence of morning. I hear him
after his shadow has passed my curtained
door. The animals and I will follow with bells
on our ankles. The cats singing love their fellows,
the dogs whispering joy.

Koana

What was the name
of the Buddha's mother?
Sublime—the story
includes trees—the Bodhi
tree, the tree that supported
her in labor, (and that cherry
tree that bent down
to give its fruit
to Mary. . .)

Did Jesus dream?
When he took his first steps
did flowers spring from the
marks? Did he ever see
himself in the mirror?
Did he see a dark face,
an ear of corn, a loaf
of braided bread, a white
camel, a donkey with
a bleeding back?

What flowers grow
in the dessert? No lotus—
what does the baby
dream, translucent eyelids
moving
before birth?

Life's Work

She set about to translate the inscriptions
beetles left under bark. This required a life
time of study. First, of course, of the various
beetles, their living metallic bodies, their hidden
wings, the hinge of lady bird wing over
lady bird back, the varied castes of spots;
then, their reproductive lives, eggs, nymphs,
molts, the favored foods, the strategies of
hunt, the carnivorous tongued, no-tongued
proboscis, the ecology of each, its niche, its
favored flights, mating time, gestation, season,
weather, humidity, wind. Disease, of course,
and the diseases of prey and their food stuffs.
And predators, their diseases, their life cycles
and sexual strategies, their bodily systems,
wastes, resources, skills. At last she achieved
the moment, magnifier at hand, the trail of
ink: it spelled nothing. It spelled all.

Lost Poem

did it begin with a wet magnolia blossom
or a cracked linoleum floor?

the incessant voice of the television
or the breath of a child asleep?

the siren, the stuck car horn
or a thrush on a city morning?

or you, the truck packed, the house empty
or the smoke from a candle snuffed out?

Long Distance

In Iranian cinema a woman and a man, even
a man and wife, may not touch, and so love
must be shown by a gaze, a downcast look,
a flutter of eyelashes shadowed on the face,
a gesture of hands, the lifting of an object
once held by the beloved, paired shadows,
reflections in a lake, a symmetry of movement
and posture; but you and I don't even have vision,
nor touch, nor scent, nor taste, and so it is voice,
tone and a subtle balance of rhythm, the way we
may repeat one another's questions, the node
of silence where our words meet, the drop to
whispers when we cannot bear to separate

Lull

Child, I would give you
the song of your making,
the tune of my breathing
the day you were born,

I will engrave the chorus
of wanting and wonder
on the cradle you rocked in
while I sang along,

I whispered the verses
when we went out walking,
I tapped out the rhythm
when we kneaded bread,

I carved out the notes
on a tree by your window,
I'll chant to your lover
on the day that you're wed,

I'll give you my rhymes
and the gift of my story,
but you'll make your own song
one morning instead.

Maiden

Yesterday my hair danced only for you.
It is brown because of your green eyes.
I have grown it to a ripe wheatfield
bristling with clicking grasshoppers
in the noonday sun. Small sweet berries
are waiting for you in its strands. They buzz
against your tongue. In Williamsburg Emily
Dickinson makes cookies in a new house.
She does not know it is a museum. My hair
does its dance for her. We bake bread.
Eldritch recipes tingle with my wheaten locks.
I grow thin as I give of myself. Surely
the city will not burn. Pickpockets are on.
The wooden locusts of yesterday wait
for my bones. The sunlight takes my
strength. You have eaten the hard crust
I threw to the dogs yesterday. Queen
of pain, princess of anger, I ride through
your bedroom on my empty breath. I will leave
you tomorrow. You will glimpse the heat
of my sweet berries baking but the house
will be empty. Dry anger pulses at the open
doors. The dogs of your youth remember your
childhood laughter. Como se llama, usted,
quantos annos tienes tu? The stone weeps
on the cold hearth. I leave only a small bag
of seeds.

The Maiden Flight of the Bumblebee / The Mating Flight of the Drone

What is the name that your father won't hear?
What does he wear in the morning?
What did he bury outside the glass door?
Why are his pockets still empty?

(The trees of the ancients were carved into spears
to battle the star of the morning
they painted the doorways with umber and lead
they tied up their hearts in bright baskets)

Who did your father dance with in April?
What music played in the hall?
Who does he bow to? Who are his masters?
What name is scarred on his neck?

(The heaviest boulders were tipped on their sides
the lichen they wore grew two faces
the bears made a cave of the mountain's reply
their skulls made a fountain in springtide)

May a River

of flowers sing for these children,
a river of honey teach them to speak,
a river of laughter teach them
to listen, a river of salt
tears teach them
to love

A memorial

Pierce my ears with fish hooks
Wire one smooth bone
Let the place be thick with lichen
Make letters of its own
(Sore that doesn't heal
Mole with a stiff black hair
Pulse beside my ear)

Who was left after all?
McGovern?
Kennedy and King dead
with the face of all people
bent over in the kitchen
the college kids all gone home

I tell my children we fell
in love with hope
Bobby Seale writes cookbooks now
Bar-B-Cue@BobbySeale.com

You will be 83
and I will find
Willie the Worm for you
and you will watch him all day
and I'll feed you strained soup
and feel such a young 75
(St. Jude,
I lost your metal.)

Imagine my rib cage strung
like a broach, like wind-chimes;
Edie's ring, my broken
wedding band, diaper pins,
thumbtacks, brass, a chain
of birds in flight, the hook
off a whiffletree,
(meadow, meadow
come home to me. . .)

Blood & Tongue 5.99/lb.

I must re-read "The Dresser of Wounds"
(How many times
did I try to speak
and the fist came down?
Even on the floor
under the kicks
my mouth keeps open.)

In Franklin people tuned in
because the-single-mother-of-twins
looked damn good
in a bathing suit.
She got voted out.
Your father got to drive
the Barbera Dodge "Flame" car
the one "Gervone," our local
survivor casualty
stands next to on the ad
with the costume-bear. . .
(I might have lost weight

or developed an appetite
for bugs. . .)

My hair two brown braids
yours thick white white white
we stood beside our bicycles
and looked across the water
the Bush compound
Kennebunkport,
it looked like Garp's place
where the Ellen Jamesians
took their empty mouths
to heal. . .

    the self is that
which divides
into good & evil
useful & empty
day & dark
live & dead
the namer,
he who makes other
of the world. . .
41

(Did you pack well?
Will you bring me something home?
Even a little bar of
soap

in Heaven's Wrapping
would be enough. . .)

I am beginning to feel
a softer heart
about the pigeon
as if one day
I might stand
like Picasso's child
with it at peace
and folded to
my breast

Myoclonus

between living and dreaming
      there is a third thing
        guess it
           Antonio Machado

in that moment when your soul drops and your body jerks
near sleep, that moment when you drift and cannot tell
how you came to be at this place, when you are aware of a great
intake of breath but do not imagine that it will leave you,
when pleasure is too much to hold or pain, there, in the warm red
dark you see them dancing, all your angels, all your demons, all
your
saints: they are small, they leave trails of light glowing
on your eyelids, their image sharpens,
they turn to face you,
they fall away,
you remain

Nobody

rocks for her baby alone
and thinks that his cry is an omen
sits on the stoop in the dark before dawn
and hopes that his breathing is normal
climbs to the top of the hill to the store
the babycart heavy and empty
waits for the family small and alone
and tells them the story of many

What is holier   than dust?

Bread   Mold
Maple seedlings   Lightning
The honey bee   The eyeless grub

Nothing

mother that was
broken
hovering kite

milk spilled
in the meadow
the sound of stones

a child's smallest
finger
the glass of
her eyes

the wheel kept
from turning
the river sung dry

the moon in your mirror
the lock on your well

the voice of a dewdrop
the failure of dawn

Pray

send me the cup
that you drank from this morning
send me the rice grains
left in your bowl

send me your comb and
the blade from your razor
send me your shoelace
send me your hair

send me the scent of your pillow this morning
send me the tears you cried in your milk

send me your scar
send me your ointment
send me your rosebud
send me your thorn

send me your sweepings
sent me your dust
 send me your moonlight
send me your song

send me the darkness you hid in your closet
the candle you stubbed out and never relit

Quake

light
the river in your eyes
your moon reflected
your childhood water
your spun glass

conscience
forgotten home
heavy hoods
bandages unwound
the bones unwrapped

covenant
sticks bundled
the woven belt, the rope
the knotted handkerchief
a braided strand of hair

truth
one stone
one leaf
frost on the window
the last wind heard

Relinquish

the tree prays
by the fallen leaf

the bird when it lines its nest
with down plucked
from its own breast

the river prays
by running dry
the stone by letting the wind
wear it down

the door prays
when it falls ajar
the hay when it surrenders to
the blade

the light when it is eaten
by darkness

the song
when it fades
away

the garden
when it is gone
past seed

the well

when it is emptied
the salmon
when it yields to
the corn

the day
when it settles
to dusk

Show us the bottom of yesterday's grief

under the highway the prophet sleeps midnight
under the river the clay turns to stone
under the lamppost the sailor keeps vigil
the doors will not open, the windows still burn

here the snake remembers the fallen
here the fawn returns from the knife
here the ambulance waits for the morning
here the jackal plays chess with the bride

the heels of her boots turned around and went clicking
the scars on her ankles repeated the sky
the flag shrouds a manikin, wrapping her head
in the wink of a tooth, in the grin of a eye

Sieve

fill me
    though I'm a vessel cracked
      and I overflow
        fill me

    though I'm a wound torn
      and a gaping mouth
        open me

    though I'm bee stung
      oozing honey
        stun me sweet

    though I am silent
      and I have no tongue
        sing through me

    though I am broken
      though I'm discarded
        make use of me

    though I am hollow
      though I hold nothing
        empty me

Study Questions

How is a child like a blade of grass?
Is regret a ringing bell? What is the duckling's
message? Is the future never spilled ink?
Who gave the arrows to joy? How is a child
like an open window? How is your mother
a frying pain? How is your father a knife?
Is memory a loaded gun? Compare and contrast
your heart with a fist. Who is the Queen
of April Street? How is a child a bullet?
What laughter does morning respect? Who
kisses the nightwind's eyes? Rewrite the chorus
of dawn. What does the winterwind mean?
If we sit in the dark does a candle speak?
Why do the boots face away from the fire?
You already knew this. How? Why does the dog
cry out with rain? Why is a feather a King?
How is the goat an injured tree? Who remembers
the hooked eel's pain? What moves the rocking
chair? Show us the number none. Discuss the meaning
 of your mother's hair. Why does the dance end
before the song? When do the stars become broken
birds? Who carries the harvest of dust? What is
the color of loneliness? "A stone carries darkness."
Explain.

Todd

It is not as I expected and then it is. As if we
only knew black and white and then there
was color so now I hear sounds in a rainbow,
the waterfalls drench my pain with the scent
of roses and peony. My darling child dances
with a ring of beautiful singers and each calls
me mother, each! Alas, I do not have the words
for it and if I did you could not hear it. I will
whisper at the edge of your photographs in
the motion of the frame, the dream shimmer that
lets the living know this world of sweet suspension
in the whirlpool of divine formless spontaneity,
this union of all we thought lost with what our
hearts wished most to find.

Tremble at

those nights when I was dropping
and I knew where I kept the knives
and I knew that I was alone
and I knew there were eight hours to morning
and night follows every dawn

those nights when I saw death
my own and I wanted to touch it
my own and I wanted to make it
my own and I knew I might do it
and night comes every day

those nights when I heard hate
and I knew that my own voice spoke it
and I knew that no one was with me
and I knew that no one else heard it
and night follows every dawn

those nights not so long ago now
when I fed myself to stop it
when I screamed at your wall to hurt us
and I drugged myself to end it
and night comes every day

and night follows every dawn
and night comes every day

"Trust the Reader"

If I make her hair red
will you read it as anger?
If she chops it off short
will you see it as flame?

If she dyes it dead black
will you wonder who hurt her?
If she grows if back long
will you think she is healed?

If I tell you she walked
everynight by the river
will you see the sky starless
or know a full moon?

Will you know who she meets
every night by the willow?
Should I tell you the name
of the one she refused?

Will you find the song wistful
of hear it as warning?
Is the sung meter steady
or awkward and odd?

Will you remember a girl
you knew once who was restless
who never found peace,
who never lay down?

Two hand sword

I was in the mechanism of the wind
   as much as the trees and the worshiping leaves
you came into the silence to teach me
   to read clouds. You said you were a cathedral
rose window slightly damaged by war
   and I saw the spiderweb torn
by too heavy prey, the weir cut
   by the pike's sharp scales,
I saw my father's photographs, Nagasaki,
   a wall still standing
pierced by light in the bomb dust
   like an eye of glass, the iris cracked to full alarm
pupil, you, archangel, you wanted light and they clothed you
   in an armor of flesh;

   I see now, at last, how you hold it
that too heavy sword, our anger, it takes both hands
   and all your concentration, how strong you are
that it so seldom falls. I would take it
   from you, like Kurosawa's wise watchmaker,
"let me carry it for a while," but I could not raise it up,
   only drag it behind me as a dangerous tail
so I watch your just pride, your dignity
   like Lou Paulmier's, the old wrestler's, when he shrugged
his rigid body against a walker
   and two canes, the lit eyes leading
the jerking neck, muscles gone to mere bandages
   for bone, and he made his broken voice
work for a moment in the meeting house

so for once even the children heard
and turned like flower faces meeting the sun
    "I stand for peace" and that broken old body
stood for us all

Waltz for Empty Arms

you were my baby girl
you were my darling world
I was yours you were mine
we had each other when. . .
now I live all alone
you grow up gone from home
and I wait all alone
in the small lamp's glow

the snow turns to rain
and the cold stays the same
I will sleep when the day
has lost meaning

you were my darling son
you were my special one
I was yours you were mine
we had each other when
I looked for time of my own
didn't know I'd be alone
now the time has grown old
and I'm slow lonely

the house breathes with dark
and the night has no end
I would welcome a hand
on the railing

you were my wanted child
you were my precious love
I was yours you were mine
we had each other when
empty days empty bed
empty face empty head
I was young I had love
call them back to me

but no footsteps will come
and the candle's burn dim
I have all I could want
but my family

Was it supposed to be

about a single dandelion seed
parachuted
against a clear blue sky?
Or a cat with a crippled leg pawing
trash
in the gutter? Or a pregnant child
sucking
her thumb in the waiting room?
Or a single blossom left after forsythia
has bloomed?

Exercise

this ladder tilts backwards
              my feet are dangling weight
I am hand over hand climbing
back into the oven of my birth

Wednesday

Why is a stone
   the girl's only hope?
Why does the father
   remarry?
What does the mother keep
   under the stove?
Discuss the refrain from
the marriage.

When did the brother
   forget to grow wings?
When did the street
   turn to butter?
Why did the meadow
   burn every spring?
Show us the bottom
of plenty.

We know earth

We swim its secret softness each day
and sleep against its bones. We are not
concerned with light but we know the scent
and taste of the rooted ones who seek it
and transform our water and dirt. We know
heat and we know the relaxation of cold
into silence. We know richness and we know
starvation in a single life. We know each other
and the wisdom of vibrations when we dance
with our starnoses tasting twilight.

Whelk

in the city of sand
we build bone house
we fear the wind
—it stings our eyes
with broken
monuments—

in the city of snow we shelter
in frozen breath—

in the salt city
we live inside our wounds
—we wait for the tongue
of our heavy god–

Who are your dead?

Who lives with your grandmother in the attic
behind your bangs? Does that kid who coughed
too much still sit under your living room couch?
Does Mr. Fairhill, the custodian, who drank
his truck through the ice still wave from behind
the mirror? Does Miss Benson run her nails
down the blackboard in your spine? And where
is that little dog? Where is Michael? Where is
the sister you once heard you might have had?
Who is that singing behind your voice on the
answering machine? And what message did
I just leave?

Why have they broken the child's hands?

Not because of night
Not because she was singing
Not because of the wolves howling from the hills

Not because of dark angels
Not because of bells falling
Not because the bats tore the flags from their poles

Not because of lost water
Not because of fever
Not because of the evening star's whine

Because she was smiling
Because she made blessing
Because the hands danced graceful in mourning

Will this one dance?

Will she carry pennies
in a broken cup? Will she cry
at a nightwindow and see dawn
spreading colors with a bird's breast
peace? Will she kiss her own forearm
and taste the sea? Will she dream
a city borrowed from tomorrow
and see, almost see, the truth?

Wind

not darkness
not dust
not the midnight siren

not the woods
not the breaking of twigs
not language, not birds

not the human
not the circle of firelight
not the black water

not alone in the church
not dancing in the churchyard
not the broken feather, not the new star

Worn

take these boots
bronze them
put them just so
in that place reserved

a epitaph will not
be needed

You are a river to our city.

The trolley changes course
to mark your birthday.
Everyone eats Italian
ices on sizzling new tar.
Tongues buzz the color pink.
Mussolini salutes you from
his monumental horse.
It is Tahiti, we eat
Tahitian treat snowcones.
No, we use the syrups
to paint your nails.
They have grown long,
a symbol of your immortality.
Mon cheri, Mon amour, Toot Sweet.
In spring the little flowers bloom:
children wear red hats.

He ain't ashamed of nothing. Sacre Blue.
The dark hounds of indiscretion bark
up your tree. Tin cans dance attendance
on your priest. You bow
to his authority. Shriven. Me, Miss
Suicidal, will learn calm.
Pretentious sidewalks await
your expedition.
Honi sant qui mal sepanse.
Fire engines bow down
to you in homage.
The trolley crosses swords
with the crosstown bus.

You wanted peaches

and I said yes
though the space was small
and shaded by a thick and knotted
tree. You wanted peaches and I believed
you could grow a tree. I trusted you to know
this climate as I am from another place
with less light, less heat. You whispered against my ear
of blossoms breathing into sunset
and I wanted to smell
the sweetness you
remembered. You spoke
and I saw the fruit hang tender
from the bending boughs, plucked, rolled cool
along the heat of my face, my sternum, down
my back. I knew the firm flesh sliced and free
pulled tart away from the stone. The bite, the stuck
ooze, the bee's hum. I trusted
your shoulders and knew just where
your shovel leaned. Years
we looked but the nurseryman had never a
peach. I argued for a cherry, a plum, a flowering
pear. And what is peach,
what is blossom, what is fruit, what is stone?
What I have is a scraggling wild rose bush
and a broken clothes pole.

Abundance

we bring the Buddha pine cones
and he sits beneath a tree
flowers, in his own garden
stones, and he is quarry
fruit, and he does not eat

we place beads to adorn
that which seeks no adornment
feathers to shadow the breathless breath
water to the source of all refreshment
words to his wise silence

how the children laughed
when Monkey somersaulted from
the Buddha's palm and pissed
on the pillar
at the end of the universe

and the Buddha showed him
the golden words on
his middle finger: "Great Sage Equaling
Heaven was here"

I try to go
I try to leave this holy space
and the Buddha brings me
what I already have
and his hand closes around me
in the fist of life

Afterword

make a rattle
    of my teeth and skull
it is not a song of celebration

grid you a screen
    of my long white hair
and set it in you window

make of my hips
    a wedding cup
salute the vinegar of forgiveness

put a single bone toe
    in your change purse
to finger before the service

take the three little bones
    from inside my ear
make you a clock that keeps ticking

click my casatanet knees
    and washboard my ribs
it is not a song of celebration